The Felon's Guide

To Integration into the Professional Society

LESSONS ALONG THE WAY

By

Tristan Buckner

"INEVITABLE"

They expect us to re enter society
Reformed and reunited with sobriety,
Unfazed by rejection—
But as to people's perception of the connection
between us and the process selection, we don't fit.
So you look at us like we'll NEVER be legit...
Some things never change.
I bet you think we don't bathe,
And I know you think we misbehave...
But did you know?
Some of us intend to grow into
Businessmen, successful and professional.
See, our wrongs some of us corrected,
Unfazed by being rejected.
In fact, we planned on it,
So instead of falling, we stand on it...
No doors we can't open.
So now that it's understood,
Well—I guess I'll see you in the neighborhood.

—Tristan
Dedicated to Daniel Lamar Reed (aka Boo Coo)

FOREWORD

BY DARRELL FREEMAN, SR.
(CEO/FOUNDER OF ZYCRON, INC.)

The prospect of living the American Dream is a birthright. The path to living this dream requires a tremendous amount of hard work, persistence, a good education and the ability to make good decisions. Unfortunately, many of us make terrible decisions that may just land us in the criminal justice system. In the blink of a bad choice, we may choose foolishly and become felons and spend years incarcerated. Tristan's book outlines how felons can live the American Dream after incarceration. Tristan teaches us that the seed for success inside of us does not die while one is incarcerated. That very seed can grow if you fertilize it with a dose of education and good decision making. It will certainly grow if you add the presence of people who not only wish you success, but have invested in it. It will most assuredly grow if you heed the words of Tristan's book.

In the book, Tristan demonstrates to us how to live life after being incarcerated. How to establish the proper mindset and what steps should be taken to get back on the path of living the American Dream. The best part is that he teaches us from his experience of becoming a successful business person, a passionate father and a contributor to his community. If you want to get on the right path read Tristan's book and the seed for success inside of you will flourish.

ABOUT THE AUTHOR

In my life I have met many people that have found themselves marginalized, disenfranchised, and ultimately on the wrong side of the law. Many never recover from this experience. Tristan Buckner flourished. Allow me to introduce you to the exception.

I was also once a young man growing up in the inner city, so it was effortless identifying with Tristan's experience and recognizing the spirit of someone like myself who refused to let these circumstances change their altitude. What a refreshing evolution.

Tristan was delivered from the harsh streets of East St. Louis to Chicago's notorious Southside in the early 90s during the deadliest times for a young black man. The crack epidemic, gun violence, Reagan Era economic strife, exceptionally high unemployment rate, and a single parent household attempted to thwart Tristan at every turn. Thankfully, that single parent was an educator who stressed the value of learning and application, and the usefulness of education. Tristan took these tools and transcended the ghetto and all the odds and made it to college. At each level, Tristan shows he is the exception to the story we have seen all too often. I am here to attest to this fact.

In 2005, I met the exception to a narrative that had played out in my mind for years. I arrived for my bi-weekly haircut appointment and I was introduced to a young man.

This young man was polite, smart, respectful, articulate and filled with hope and dreams. Over the next few years, I learned that this same exceptional young man that I had taken a special interest in was a convicted felon.

However, it never changed how I saw Tristan. I asked him about his journey and I learned that he is like many other young people in search of success in America. During this expedition he found himself confronted with a crossroad that would ultimately alter his destination: an altercation that led to him spending the next 13 years in prison. Not only did his journey change him. It also changed me. Spending the last 11 years as a client of Tristan's Barbershop I've learned so much about myself and the opportunity to give people a real chance. I've watched a leader emerge from his experience and a determination to help others. What endeared me to Tristan wasn't just his story, but his desire and the work ethic to realize those hopes and dreams. Tristan wishes not only to use his tools to support himself, but to build a legacy that transcends the label once applied to him. He is an entrepreneur in every sense and I recognized him in spirit.

Our society has taught us to fear the unknown and to not give a so-called felon a chance at success and happiness. I challenge you to do what I have had the privilege to do for the last 11 years and that is to sit and read from a changed man to an emerging leader. Tristan's words will speak louder than the words on the page. They will tell a story that needs telling.

~ Louis Upkins, Entrepreneur & Author
Treat Me Like a Customer: Using Lessons from Work to Succeed in Life

THANK YOU!

———————

I would like to Thank God for giving me the knowledge and understanding throughout my journey to share what I was blessed to learn. I'd like to thank Ms. Buckner... (Moma) you've stood by me since day one, and it would take a volume 6 to express it on paper. Just know "I got you". Loren, Ben (RIP) Big Brother, and all my family... Love Y'all.

To those whose busy lives may have made them forget their deeds, just know that I haven't! Special Thanks to: Jim Cosby (Former Assistant Commissioner), honestly you opened the door of opportunity to make this materialize. George Little (Former TDOC Commissioner) and Kirt Sarago (Former IRC).

To my mentors, guides, and examples of what life can be. You all came in at various phases of my life, yet all of the pieces of the puzzle came together as it was destined to be. Mr. Darrel Freeman Sr., Dr. Victor Anderson, Mrs.Glinda Lingo, Dr. Janice Wolff, Ms. Chitoka Webb, Mr. Asa Briggs, Mr. Lewis Upkins, Dr. Catana Starks, Jeff Hassel & Coach (BCCC), Trillion Smalls, and Brenda McClearen who made it "happen".

As for Tristan's Barbershop clients, I've learned from you all... Thank you all! It truly does take a village; now I know for a fact!

~ **Tristan Buckner, Author**

CONTENTS

INTRODUCTION

Felony: a crime punishable by death or imprisonment in excess of one year.

This is a guide for felons, laying out the basics of starting and maintaining professional relationships.

Once a person is labeled a felon, he or she is ushered into a parallel universe in which discrimination, stigma, and exclusion are perfectly legal, and privileges of citizenship such as voting and jury duty are off limits. It does not matter whether you have spent time in prison; your second–class citizenship begins the moment you are branded a felon. Most people branded felons, in fact, are not sentenced to prison. As of 2008, there were approximately 2.3 million people in prisons and jails, and a staggering 5.1 million people under "community correctional supervision" -- i.e., on probation or parole.[1]

I have experienced these conditions. Luckily I'm in a position to use my experiences to better myself, and hopefully other felons. While doing business with blue and whitecollar workers, professional athletes, and musicians for the last decade, I've learned by trial and error to work with leaders.It can be a complex circumstance for a felon who does not have the slightest idea how he or she might be accepted in a world that says, "You no longer matter." But the truth is you do belong! You matter!

A friend, pivotal in my development as a professional in

the hair industry, once told me, "We have all benefitted from someone else's labor. Now it is important that I live in such a way that someone can learn from my experience. I am now responsible for guiding someone else's steps because so many other people were responsible for guiding mine."[2]

From gaining clients to losing clients and rebuilding my clientele all over again, to dealing with professionals, I've realized that there are many different facets to being prepared for things to come after being released from jail. Especially when you carry a label: FELON.

In some cases we get out, thinking we are prepared. So many of us still have to climb over walls of fear. What I have learned and experienced comes with limits. It took ten years for me to break through the many barriers I had constructed. There were many lessons that I wish someone would have prepared me, for but I had to learn those hard lessons on my own. In this booklet is a small sampling of the many lessons I have learned along the way; while traveling from felon to becoming an entrepreneur. The lessons presented in this guide have had measurable results in all aspects of my professional journey.

1 Michelle Alexander, (New York;New Press, 2012) The New Jim Crow: P.94 (PEW Center for the States, One in 31.)

2 Chitoka Webb, Something Inside of Me (Austin, TX: Emerald Book Co., 2011), 151.

1

STRIVE TO BE YOUR BEST

Strive for success. Accept who you are, who you can become, and be more forgiving of yourself, because everybody makes mistakes. Don't hide who you 'can be' by settling for the stereotypically depicted life of a felon. Challenge yourself. Continue your education, whether in prison or picking up where you left off prior to your incarceration.

*****WARNING*****

FAILURE IS TOO EASY

2

THE PAST IS YOUR 'STEPPING STONE'

———————

Be mindful that most people have never come face to face with a felon. Levels of exposure to felons can be very different in every community, and each encounter. **REMEMBER:** It's **your** choice to decide who you choose to share the details of your life story. Be wise. Make smart choices regarding who you trust with your past choices. Not everyone is trustworthy or deserving of 'your truth' as a felon.

To my knowledge, only job applications require you to say whether you have ever been convicted of a felony; which has been recently changed in some states (thanks to President Obama). If you live in a state that has yet to change the law, you can put the phrase, "Will discuss upon interview" on the applications. That will give you the opportunity to explain your situation; because each situation is unique.

Once you've decided to tell someone about your past, be sure it is someone who has respect for the person you are *now*. If you recite your life story to everyone you meet, put the emphasis on the person you have now become through your efforts, time, life lessons and, more importantly, with God's intervention.

Contrary to how the LIKE button operates on Facebook, in nonvirtual society, once you LIKE someone it's hard to UNLIKE them simply because of their history. Treat others the way you would want to be treated: with empathy, compassion, and hopefulness. Once they see that in you, you can expect high returns. Remember, if you want to change how people think about felons you are the agent of change. Build trust by being trustworthy.

While in prison I was blessed to be a part of a work release program that reintroduced me to civil society each day. While being locked up, a wise woman told me, "God trusts you in the position you're in. It has nothing to do with me; by God trusting you, people will follow suit." If your priorities are in order, people look at your life as being in order.

3

DON'T WEAR YOUR RECORD ON YOUR COLLAR

Many people champion their past incarceration as if they received the Heisman trophy. They strut like a prize boxer having just secured the world championship. Other felons are tempted to brag about their incarceration for a number of reasons. They may be seeking attention, recognition, or respect on the streets. Truth be told, being incarcerated because of one's poor decisions and actions is nothing to brag about. While learning from your past, focus on reclaiming your future. Instead of bragging or boasting, it is good to keep in mind this scripture, "Whatsoever things are true, whatsoever things are honest, whatsoever things are of good report; if there be any virtue, and if there be any praise, think on these things. Those things, which you have both learned, and received, and heard, and seen in me, do: and the God of peace shall be with you." (Philippians 4:8-9). If you keep this in mind, and practice it, you will earn the respect of others.

4

COMMUNITY MATTERS

———————

Get active in your community. Use your knowledge and past experiences to improve the world around you. When people are acquainted with your good character, and respect you for your service, they most likely will treat you accordingly.

There are people from all walks of life who live every day helping others. As a result they have learned that life goes beyond themselves. In prison many felons develop a selfish outlook on life and feel that their situation is more significant than others. It turns into the 'I' and 'Me' mindset. Felons with this mindset have not yet learned that 'while it was *Me* who got *Me* into *My* situation, it takes All of Us to help Me get out of My situation'. I am speaking from a place of experience. I was a financial burden to my family at the beginning of serving my sentence. The phone call rates were so high, that consistently calling collect to my family had the *phone disconnected in no time. It took the "community" of inmate families to protest the extreme pricing of phone calls over a period of time to make it a relevant issue.*

5

CIRCLE OF HOPE

Acquire a positive circle of friends and acquaintances whose professions and life backgrounds differ from yours. You've already wasted enough time with individuals who have shown you their dark side and connected with yours. It is time to surround yourself with people who can reboot your mind and direct your life positively on *what* to do and *how* to do it, in a healthy, positive way. "As iron sharpens iron, so one person sharpens another." (Proverbs 27:17)

When you live life with a purpose you learn quickly YOU CAN'T DO IT ALONE, this is your opportunity to get out to mixers, gatherings, and other social events that put you in a position to meet people in different professions as well as socioeconomic levels. To what extent you become involved in one another's purpose, will only be known once you choose to take the first step towards change and SPEAK. Let your newfound peers and friends not intimidate you as a person or professional, let their success and the exposure they offer be your drive to want more in life.

6

DEVELOP IDEAS

———————

Whatever ideas you have held in the past, or currently hold, don't let them go. Write them down, think them through, compile them, and find a mentor (there are many mentor programs offered to felons). Writing your ideas down is helpful. Trying to remember all of them can be tricky. While developing your dreams, writing them down will also help you determine what you can achieve. Your goal, along with your mentor will determine the ideas that are possible to bring to fruition.

Once you've narrowed your ideas, do the legwork. Research everything. It's all there, at your fingertips. The internet can be a felon's, or anyone's, best colleague and friend in developing ideas.

7

MENTAL HEALTH

———————

Fearing of mental health issues or denial can be a common thought process amongst individuals not treating abnormal behavior; when most deem it as common behavior. After being incarcerated for a period of time, you probably had witnessed or had taken part in violent acts and tense situations. Most likely you have been in a survivalmode of thinking, and experienced emotional numbness. Your experience could be equivalent to a tour of duty, but outside the military structure. PTSD, bipolar, and anxiety disorders can occur after experiencing trauma, such as a life of incarceration. You may want to contact a qualified professional, such as a therapist. Be open and transparent about your past with these trained professionals so that you can get insight into your problems and anxiety. After a period of freedom outside of bars, I had the opportunity to visit a mental health professional, let down my guard and revisit my past. After a few sessions and reviews, I was diagnosed with PTSD and slight Bipolar symptoms. I tried the medicated remedy, and not to hinder any ones treatment choice, but I chose God over the pills. Some people need both. But ALL need God.

If you want to be effective in whatever you do, you need to conduct a selfinterrogation. If there are any issues and problems not dealt with, address them ASAP! Then take the first step forward.

8
RELATIONSHIPS

Domestic violence is one of the top reasons why men return to prison. Felons on parole or on probation are held to a "zero tolerance" policy. Whether innocent or guilty, you will be locked up and sent back to jail; pending the outcome of your case. You stand to lose everything that you have worked hard to redeem in your life, your employment (if you can't show up to work), your apartment/home/car (if you can't pay rent/payments). Most importantly, you will relinquish the trust of people who believed in you (or you'll burn the bridges you spent time building).

Be mindful that a toxic relationship for a felon on parole is like kryptonite to Superman. You will lose your strength and become susceptible to a return – AND NOT TO HOME, my friend!

Watch for more information on this topic in:

THE FELON'S GUIDE
TO BUILDING RELATIONSHIPS (VOLUME 4)

Coming soon.

9

A HIGHER POWER

We were not created to do life alone. That is why it is important for you to build a spiritual foundation. Sometimes we think once we make it out of prison we can get by on our efforts alone. In reality, we couldn't have done it without the help of our Higher Power. *Prayer became a tool to my peace of mind while in prison. I've prayed standing, I've prayed prostrating, I've prayed laying down, with my eyes open and shut, and I can honestly say that God has guided me in each and every setting of praise.*

We are blessed to have another chance when so many won't get that opportunity... EVER! Remember: you didn't do it alone, and you never will get anything done to its full potential, alone. When you initially got locked up, you would have prayed to a toilet if you honestly thought it could help you get out. Recognize your need for your Higher Power.

10
MOVING ON

Your past is important, but dwelling on it can keep you from moving forward with your personal and professional goals, and keep you stuck in the past. Move on! Discover the limits of your life skills, target areas for growth, and take small steps. This will build your self-confidence but dream big. This will help keep you inspired. Let your vision guide your every step. Remember, moving ahead is a lifetime project. Stay focused on the priorities of your life: you, family, and your professional goals.

11

CONSTRUCTIVE CRITICISM

———————

Felons often look at getting out of prison as being fresh out of a controlled environment where they have gotten accustomed, as a lifestyle, to neither asking or answering too many questions. Being accountable to oneself alone may give felons the illusion that they know it all and are not accountable to others. I realized that you have to LEARN to help. What you know makes you who you are, what you learn molds you into who you want to be. We are accountable to one another; so listen, learn, and then teach.

Remember: You are no longer in that environment. Being open to constructive criticism is a critical key to your personal and professional success. Keep your ego and temper in check when offered constructive criticism. Others you meet have experience, knowledge, skills and wisdom that you will need to advance your own ideas and vision. That is why it's great to be open to others point of view.

12

MIND YOUR OWN BUSINESS

The numberone rule of prison, and business, is *"Mind your own business"*. It is far too easy to get distracted from cultivating habits you will need for establishing your professional success by comparing yourself to others, or living with selfdoubt. Cultivate virtues, or habits that will keep you thriving personally and professionally. Be selfaware of what you can or can not do. Everyone has limits in skills, knowledge, and finances. Be positive about the image you want to cultivate and portray about you as a person and professional. A sense of class and taste go a long way toward enhancing your profession and character. Be time conscious. Time is not only money; it is also a precious commodity. Respect how you spend your own time and respect the time of others. Persevere! There are a lot of haters out there. You will be tested by selfdoubt or by peer envy. But always persevere. Persevere means hold on and stay the course. You will earn the respect of those closest to you and your potential clients. Customers will maintain faith and confidence in you.

13
CULTURE MATTERS

It is a great asset for one to learn not only about one's own culture in business, but also to learn about other cultures. Such learning broadens one's horizons. **It's interesting to learn about those with different beliefs, rituals, and lifestyles. It has opened my mind to new ways of thinking and living, as well as cleared up a lot of misunderstandings that we have in the world about people of different cultures and choices. Realize there is more than one way to do something by thinking outside the box.** Be open to new foods, places, and people different than yourself. The world is big; make it your mission to experience as much of it as possible. People are creatures of habit. Many stick with what they know and with what they are most comfortable. Experiencing life and learning about other cultures help you to remember that life is bigger than a bed next to a toilet.

14
FULL SPEED AHEAD

———————

Focus on your future goals. Be mindful that it's okay to ask for help, guidance, and direction. Devote time mapping out your steps and goals. It will help keep you on track, and give you a realistic time frame in which to complete the necessary steps to reach the finish line. Use your new circle of friends as accountability partners. Choose people who will ask questions to provoke thought, as well as help monitor your progress; which may help battle procrastination tendencies. The next time you encounter your circle of healthy friends, share with them your development and steps getting started and finish the job.

*****

I hope you found these professional lessons helpful, and that you take them to heart. As a felon, I know what you're going through, and I am also continuously progressing toward improving my own life. There are more helpful lessons along the way in my following booklets. May God bless you on your new journey toward reentering civil society as you become a productive and positive citizen!

UPCOMING BOOKS FROM
THE 'FELON'S GUIDE' SERIES:

THE FELON'S GUIDE
TO AVOIDING THE PITFALLS THAT RETURN
YOU TO INCARCERATION (volume 2)

THE FELON'S GUIDE
TO BALANCING FAMILY,
NEW FRIENDS & OLD FRIENDS (volume 3)

THE FELON'S GUIDE
TO BUILDING RELATIONSHIPS (volume 4)

THE FELON'S GUIDE
TO STARTING YOUR OWN BUSINESS (volume 5)

– NOTES & QUESTIONS –

– NOTES & QUESTIONS –

– NOTES & QUESTIONS –

www.ingramcontent.com/pod-product-compliance
Lightning Source LLC
Chambersburg PA
CBHW071439040426
42445CB00012BA/1394